a paige in
my diary

a paige in my diary

words by

paige cary

paige cary self publishing
los angeles, california 90006
paigecary.com

ISBN: 978-0-5786-3454-8

editor: chanelle a. watson
art designer: phoebe landolt (ig: @bewell_livefree)
cover illustration: phoebe landolt (ig: @bewell_livefree)

c o n t e n t s

for
my mother,
my father,
and my brother.
thank you, for never giving up on me.

the
suffering...

we have been taught silence
keep your experiences to yourself
and keep your mind in check
we have been taught
what has happened to us
deserves nothing other than
silence
so we suppress
we ignore the begging in our mind to speak up
can you even know for sure that it has happened
since you are not speaking
now i am consumed with a foggy memory
searching for every last detail
years of silence
who were you
wait
there were two of you
i think i remember
good
keep silent

young and fiercely curious
discovering my sex
i was too young
discovering sex
innocence stripped away
being lost in sex
i was too young

i ask to go
heart pounding in my chest
but you say no
the both of you
say no
where was i supposed to go
if i was told no

disconnected from myself
i wandered looking for answers
my body no longer belonging to me
but to every man

she was deep like the oceans
ready to crash from a force larger than herself
swallowing up the lives of the ones
who dare to push themselves to her deep end
she refuses to spit them back out
since they have now made a home out of her

i lost my virginity.
i don't understand what sex is.
i didn't want to have my virginity taken.
i had my virginity ripped away from me by the two of you.
i don't know if sex is supposed to feel good,
i will remain numb down there.
thirteen.

i thought i went through this already.
i stopped giving myself to others.
i found you,
i liked you,
and you liked me.
i was convinced to see you that night by your comforting
words.
i told you, i had to focus on schoolwork.
i told you, to stop kissing me.
i told you, i did not want to be touched.
i told you, i was serious.

you stopped,
you said you were sorry.
you were good with words.
you listened to me complain about school.
you watched *family guy* with me.
you cuddled me and said you cared for me.

you watched me fight my exhaustion.
you watched me sleep.
you woke me with your cold fingers in me.
you slid yourself in me.
you never looked at me.
you finished.

i did nothing.
i could not find my voice.
i tried to squirm from under your weight.
i still did nothing.
i waited for you to finish.

i watched you turn for sleep now.
i waited to move from next to you.
i left you behind.
i left that night behind at,
nineteen.

sex requires acknowledgement
one person has said *no*
one person has not given the magic word of *yes*
and the other person ignores those obvious indications
and the other person does not consider the emotions of the
person they are dealing with
and the other person continues to place themselves inside of
a sacred space where they are unwelcomed
it can no longer be referred to as sex
it is nothing other than
rape
abuse
and sexual assault

how could i tell anyone this big of a burden
voices collapsing into one another
asking question after question
too many questions
with no room for an answer to tumble out
who would believe me when i say i am
just as confused as they are
they would want to know why i waited
so long to say something
they would want to know why i waited so long to speak up
all the while i want to know why it happened twice

your rape will shift something inside you
and leave you to pick up the pieces
but believe me when i say
there will be more days ahead for you

i met my worst enemy at thirteen years old,
the two of us had a love hate relationship.
she required the kind of attention
you would rather be free of,
she knows exactly how to pierce herself into my skin,
sharp with her used edges.
as much as i wanted to leave this relationship,
i kept going back for more.
i needed to feel my skin cry against hers,
to see her open me,
while the red tears released out of me.
the moment she saw those tears is when she disappeared.
leaving me to get rid of her mess,
forced to act as if she never existed.

a daughter
who wanted to ask for help
but did not know how
who knows her family will help
but cannot be seen as weak
who breaks the rules
who wants to be heard
who wants to explain why she is the way that she is
who wants to be the best she can be
this only led her down a road of self-destruction
instead
this daughter swallows herself whole

examining my dark skin with a sense of curiosity
trying to look at myself without cringing
at the eyes that glare back
they bore into my flesh as i silently wish
i could look at anything other than this reflection

when she asks for reassurance
he pumps hate into her mind
like the idea of her wanting more
is too much to bare on his own
so he puts her on the back burner
like he does everything else

i cannot stop looking at others with envy behind my eyes.
i am allowing my mind to run wild
with the self-loathing thoughts.
i am beginning to repeat what was
told to me in high school.
you are dark,
you are ugly,
you are nothing.
looking at the girls with lighter skin
and how the boys wanted something good from them,
this dark skin never got that sort of gratitude,
this dark skin became a young boy's secret desire,
nothing that can be taken seriously.
covering the true complexion with as
much beauty standards as possible,
there has to be something i can do to get one shade lighter.
all you have to do is direct me to that unknown place
that allows me to strip myself clean of this skin,
tell me which way must i go.

sometimes it's the most silent individuals
who have the loudest minds
expressing what storm is forming within
would only validate that there is something wrong
who wants to look in the eyes of a woman
who constantly shies away from herself
actually that is not the question
who has the patience for a woman
who refuses to see herself
there has to be one person who will turn that
woman's face around when she retreats
to simply say
show me who you are
despite her flaws
there has to be a man for that woman
despite her flaws
there has to be a woman for that woman
but as that storm settles in
can that woman recognize the
difference of those two beings
while they firmly stand in the eye of her storm
that woman needs reassurance
but more importantly unconditional love
anyone can say they love you when
the moment seems right
but that does not mean they can handle
the capacity of loving someone other than themselves

you are a reflection of your mother
with a smile that becomes contagious
the moment you give yourself to others
but that silence you have learned to embrace
belongs to your father

daddy,
you are one of the most fascinating creatures
that has been placed upon this earth.
i want you to understand me but i
want to understand you more.
sometimes when you call, i want you to
tell me what is on your mind
far beyond the walls that others don't get to see.
instead,
i enjoy bonding over the little things that brighten my day.
like our thoughts on the many shows
that have been binged over time.
i want you to know i appreciate all that
you have done for our family,
you give and give without expecting any sort of return.
i no longer blame you for not knowing
how to be soft with me,
there are times that i disappear with
my thoughts and wonder
what it is that makes you lose track of time.
my skin is your skin with less life worn onto it.
i am your daughter.
i will always be a daddy's girl.
i now know how much you love me
and want me to be okay,
i never want you to go a day without
knowing how much you mean to me.

you made me feel something i never felt towards another girl
for the most part i am ignoring that feeling
because that would mean something i knew nothing about
at least not yet
we were painting our nails while the radio buzzed
quietly in the background
we were home alone
and that is when you asked me
if i had ever kissed a girl
my surprised expression
gave my answer away
immediately
you move closer to me
kiss me on the lips
and hesitation wrapped its weight around us
then we allowed our lips to explore each other
losing track of what swept away from us
i liked it

i can't tell if i like girls
or not
or if i like boys more
whatever this feeling is
do not share it with anybody

i let them touch me
so i can feel anything
constantly searching for more
getting nothing in return
but still i needed the sex

i told you i liked kissing you
but i wanted it to stay between us
you promised
and that is when i knew that i could trust you

i thought that i could trust you then,
besides it was you that was left on my mind
while my eyes fluttered shut for the night.
exploring our sacred world's at such a delicate age,
kissing behind closed doors all while
promising to keep it our dirty little secret.
but there was a day that i lost my trust in you for good.
when you left me alone with the both of them.
we wanted to be greeted by mary jane herself
and they knew where to find her.
we were younger than them
and they could smell the purity that rested upon our skin.
wanting nothing more than to make it their own,
i could sense their hunger,
as you could sense their hunger too.
i was ready to go
but the toilet was calling for a visit.
i said goodbye to that disheveled bathroom

wanting to see nothing of it again
and that is when reality tapped me on the shoulder,
you were gone while they remained.
you ignored my texts,
you ignored my calls,
you were never as oblivious as i
and these two snakes knew of you but nothing of me.
you left just in time to miss their venom strike
through the core of my innocence.
you all had power over me.
you left me while they ripped me
apart from the inside out,
did you know they would attack that day?
did you know that they would rape me?
at the same time
i trusted you
and i thought i liked you
and thought i liked girls too.

to every person who has been
sexually harassed,
groped,
molested,
assaulted,
or raped,
i want you to know that my heart beats with yours.
i promise you that myself
and so many others stand behind your experience.
my story is valid
and your story is valid.
my pain is real
and your pain is real.
my voice deserves to be heard
and so does yours.
if you are ashamed and feel as though
you are unable to use your voice,
that is okay.
nobody has the power to make you
speak out if you are not ready to.
period.

there is no time limit for the healing process.
continue to take every single day
one day at a time,
we survived the worst
and we can only grow from here.
some may think that speaking out
about rape culture is a lost cause
but i disagree on too many levels.
we cannot continue to condone that
sort of thinking anymore,
it is a new day
and survivors will no longer be silenced.
quit justifying the actions of the people who
can violate another person's boundaries,
we do not care about what you have to say,
it will always be wrong.
stand with survivors.
the only way a difference will become a reality
is when victim-blaming is no more.
there is power in numbers,
so stand with me and the beautiful people
who have gone through trauma.
and to my darlings who have gone through any of this,
ME TOO.

emptying out my memory of any
lingering reminders of your existence
was the first act of
dismissing that day of misfortune

learning to forget the world
you introduced me to
was the second act of
hiding my sexuality

hearing that you told others of our secret,
about my identity,
about my interest in girls along with boys
that was the final act of
falling deep into denial

you couldn't handle my request
of love
of acceptance
of appreciation
i decided you were right
i had too many needs
i needed to be loved by you
but you refused to see me that way

she is the kind of girl
that constantly searches for the wrong attention
she allows all the wrong eyes
to get a glimpse of the pages that fill her story
yet she has never once realized how
undeniably
irresistible
she really is

the
colliding...

despite your lack of concern
my heart still beats for you
crazy to think that after all you put me through
i still wonder how you are doing
but that is what you call love
and i love with my entire being
while i know i am not easy to love at times
i also know that true love is hard to find
we cross paths with people for a reason that is beyond us
the universe knows what the stars have aligned for us
which means at any given moment
our story can abruptly end
just like that
nothing more and nothing less
and that is exactly what happened
you left when you promised that love was on your mind
you made promises that were impossible to keep
i know it is easy for you to walk away from your word
but believe me when i say
all i really hope is that you are doing okay

i forgive you
i love you
and i miss you

know that there is a
difference between
loving someone
and being completely in love with someone
still i find myself searching
for what it was when i looked at you

i appreciated you for reminding me
that it is okay to
like who i like
i appreciated you for being the one
to unlock the barricaded door that
protected my hidden secret
i appreciated you for
allowing me to be me

you probably remember it too
how the rest of the world
slept their day away behind us
while we remained awakened by our inebriated words
watching the stars fade into the next day
never considering the end of a friendship
that could have lasted a lifetime
instead your confession seemed more appealing to fall for
not once did we look back from there
but we managed to run like hell
with zero consideration towards
what we just put ourselves in

you made it so easy
to love you
your spirit
your laugh
your compassion for others
your compassion for me
never could i have imagined
falling for someone like you

nothing felt more like home
than her legs wrapped around my own
protecting me from my thoughts
without even realizing the affect she had on me

i know you have your own insecurities
for reasons you believe i am unaware of but have you heard
the words that drop out of my mouth
when i remind you that
you are my person

your skin is covered with all the broken
promises engraved by the others
most of the time you cannot look at the
skin you live in with a smile
i can see that you are afraid of who you are
but i have never been turned off by any of that
why don't you believe me when i tell you i see you
why don't you believe me when i
tell you that i do need you
i am not the only damaged one here
i am not the only one that wants to be seen
we are both a mess but i was willing to push
through your treacherous storms

i am who i am
i am a ticking bomb ready for explosion
but you swear you are prepared for the aftermath

she has come home to unconditional love
flowers waiting to be held at the kitchen table
letters reminding her that her presence
meant more to me than i know i put out
still this was my acknowledgement
that i was in this for the long run

she says
you don't love me the way i love you
i look at her with a blank expression
she waits for my response
but she never hears the reassurance
she is desperately in search for
to me she is disregarding
the ways i show
love and affection

i had thoughts of walking away from you
i knew things would never be the same
friends then lovers
both held too much meaning
to walk away so easily

i wonder if you can fall in love too quickly
and i think the answer is yes

love takes patience
love takes acceptance
love takes dedication
love takes honesty
and above all
love takes two people
who are willing to be there
when the other needs to
learn from mistakes
now ask yourself
if this is what you want
with that other person

maybe facing my past demons
that lived in each corner of
my exhausted mind
changed the course of our relationship

maybe sharing every worry with you
made you look the other way

maybe i could have dealt with
the reality of my rape
before we agreed to fall into one another
besides it was not your job to fix me
that was my own duty
but as my partner
it was your job to speak up
when you could no longer handle much more

dealing with a partner who has
anxiety
depression
post traumatic stress disorder
and trichotillomania
is a lot of pressure for one person
i do apologize a million times
for the confusion you must of felt
on how to help me

your soulmate is somewhere out there
and when he or she steps into your life
that love will be overwhelmingly fresh
that love will leave you at a loss of words
there will be times when that love
leaves you disappointed
but that love will be redeemable
because a soulmate knows
how life has its moments

do you ever think about what we had
and thought that it is not worth losing
i do because
i wonder if you have moments of regret
when you think about how it all ended

you have touched me plenty of times
without me flinching away
but it was the way you touched me
that one time that placed me back in time
the time when i was nineteen
without a voice to say no
without a voice to say stop
your fingers inside me
sent chills down my spine
leaving me paralyzed once again
it was when i looked at you
that i saw him instead
you stopped when you saw the flood of tears escape my eyes
afraid that it was you that caused this unexpected eruption
instead of asking if i was okay
you held me in your arms and allowed me to melt away
that moment changed how i saw you
it made me love you even more
but it meant the end was soon approaching for you

i lost myself
my sensuality nowhere to be found
and there was no way to bring it back
i lost myself
my lack of intimacy was apparent
when i no longer called for your touch
i lost myself
my body no longer recognizable
to my own weary eyes

get a drop of liquor in me
and suddenly i need you
to feel me in all the places
that make me crumble

on the days that are not filled with
uncertainty towards what lies ahead for us
should be reminders that
everything is temporary

you taught me that i cannot control every situation
and to appreciate the time that we did have together
even if it was not as long as we both anticipated
the universe has a plan for us that
expands further than our own imagination
no day goes by where i do not think
about how you are doing
or if you have found happiness in all that life has to offer
you were the most challenging yet exceptional
lesson i had the honor of discovering
even if i may be alone in these feelings
i have accepted that reality
for all the places you may go in life
i pray that you move into it with grace and patience

when you say you love someone
make sure you know how much weight that word holds
love is not something to mess around with
if you are not ready for it
love is powerful and can change a person
if the love that you give to someone is returned
be careful as to not let that go for it is rare to come by
we are humans who are eager to
experience love in all ways possible
forgetting that love is supposed to be
natural and wholehearted
love is not supposed to hurt
so think about that the next time
you decide to give your love to another

and when the sun slips past the moon
to prepare for her daily descent
i wonder if there is a hint of jealousy
as the moon rises with all the protection
from her stars spread across the concealed sky

but the one person that we forget
who needs the most intense kind of love
is the one that we shy away from too often
and that is ourselves

i deserve someone
who understands what it means
to hurt on the inside as i have
felt that ache at a young age
i deserve someone
who will hold my hand
even if i let go each time
i feel fingers intertwined with my own
this is the type of person
who gives without any expectation
of receiving anything in return
before i even realize it
this person will put me above all
while still pushing to grow deeper within themselves
even when there are no words passing between us
the person i deserve will be content with the silence
from a man or a woman
i refuse to settle for you

we have been away from each other for a few months. not like the beginning of our relationship when we had to wait for you to be in the same city. this time i am away from you to better myself. it has gotten to the point that i am incapable of managing my mental health on my own. my depression is suffocating me with no release, while my anxiety leaves me a prisoner to my own body. the tension is running high between us because i am impossible to love like this. so i told you i am leaving our life and you behind to face my trauma. the time is now. i love you so much but i am through with being the cause of this friction. it is time to face my past and work on myself. not just for me though, for us too. i want to move past this bump in the road that i know is not forever. we agreed that this would be a test to the relationship but you promised to stay to see me on the other side.

i wish you could see how hard i am fighting for my life. not being able to look away from myself is torture. my family checked me into an outpatient program. no days off when it comes to recovery. i am exhausted beyond belief. i can sense your hesitancy but i cannot figure out why it is there. you tell me you love me. you tell me you are proud of my strength. you tell me you cannot wait for me to come home to you. these are baby steps but progress for the both of us.

i just completed my first round of treatment. i am coming home to you a day early to surprise you. this is the happiest i felt in a long time. there is a weight that has been removed from my shoulders. a month and a half of pure isolation besides the love and support of family and close friends with me at home. i am coming home to you as a new person.

i know you are proud of me. but that is when i get a call from you. eager to hide the secret of seeing you the next day from my voice, it was your voice that stopped me mid-sentence. something about your tone shot my heart out of my chest. i kept asking what was wrong and that is when you said you needed to talk. my mind racing with all that i could have done wrong. nothing. it was then that you told me you were done with me. you said the moment i left that you tried but just like i left to get my happiness back you found your happiness the moment you did not have to see me. i begged. i swore i was a better person. i apologized for falling into the darkness from my rape. reminding you that i left everything behind to better myself. more begging with you refusing to change your mind. i did not get better soon enough. you said it was too late. that was that.

devastated was an understatement. this was my fault. if i never got raped at thirteen and nineteen none of this would be happening. i would be a normal girl. all alone with my thoughts. this is all too much. calling one friend telling her that this was it and shut my phone off. now looking my enemy in the eye after years of separation and brought her keen body to my own. i was ready to go. so i cut deep without thinking.

i feel nothing. i hear nothing until my name is being screamed piercing through my ears. it is the woman who carried me for nine months. the woman who would trade her life for me to breathe. blood streaming down my wrists as i collapse into her arms. my father now behind her. a look plastered across his face that i have never seen before. fear of losing his little girl. my world crashing down on my shoulders all because you made me feel like this was all my fault. it was my friend who saved me by calling my brother. it was my brother who called 911 from another state. you are nowhere to be found. gone for good like you wanted.

three months later i managed to survive being hospitalized. three months later i managed to survive a longer round of outpatient treatment. and three months later i finally can look at myself and say i made it here on my own without you beside me. baby girl. i want to thank you for leaving me the way that you did. i want to thank you for showing me what fake love looks like. the love that i needed has been there for me all along and you were never it. so i want to take a moment to give thanks to those who stuck by my side in my darkest of moments. it is these people who knew i would survive my saddest days.

so thank you a million times and more to:

moma daddy chase uncle darryl chloe evan
aunt judy granny rea aunt lorna aunt
nadine aunt sidni nana d
cousin eric amanda amandalyn sammie averie xandy kaya
jazmin drew michelle

unconditional love has been with me all along.

the
wandering...

nobody quite warns you
how lonely it can be
to have nothing
but your thoughts
to hold you steady

everyone around me is telling me
that i am wasting my time
the truth is i am just living in denial
that it is actually over
but i just need to see you
because maybe then you will remember
remember what i meant to you
before we found ourselves here
my mother
my father
and my brother
all staring at me with torn away looks
knowing that this was a battle
that only i could overcome

my heart collapsed inside my chest
towards your final goodbye

i ripped out the pages of my diary
one glimpse at the memories
that slowly consumed me
one day at a time
never getting the chance
to be seen in between these lines again
forever a ghost to what i thought i knew

i know what i need
yet it is your dishonesty that i crave
i have become used to
your words of encouragement
that meant nothing to you

so how will i tell the difference
when the person that i deserve
shows me the same as you once did

paige cary

last night
the sky tried to guide you home
by igniting life into your eyes
i cursed at the stars
for even getting a glimpse of you

i lay in bed
with zero urge
to leave these sheets
that once belonged to you
my legs spread apart
in search of your fingers
marking their territory
along these rigid walls
and still you are not here
i would rather slip out of my skin
than not have you wrapped around me

how many days have gone by
since we hugged goodbye
each day and each night
blending into one another
i am no longer in control of myself
my thoughts crippling
my insides with no release
you have to come back home
eventually
but we know the collision of our worlds
were meant to happen once in this lifetime

you have made me hate every piece of you
no
i mean none of that
you are a stranger
i long to reintroduce myself to
yes
i think we met each other at the wrong time
maybe
the day will come
where i hear your name
and i can be left with a smile instead of regret

i can forgive you
but do you carry any remorse
no
for that you will remain
as a distant memory

people do what they want to do
if you meant something to her
she would have stood by you
while the rain drenched your
worn down body with its toxicity
a rainbow is never far behind
once a storm has drifted pass
realize that you were never
the root of this madness
you see you were the colors
that stopped people in their tracks
to admire such a calm beauty

do we ever pay attention
to our own wants and needs
the deeper we fall in a relationship
at what point do we forget
to see if we are doing okay
above anything and anyone else
do we care to have control
over our own desires

paige cary

even on the days
that left us disgusted
with each other
i will be the one
that got away for good
whatever mattered more
friendship or lover
you will never find the same

i made the mistake
of begging for forgiveness
as if the road to healing past wounds
had everything to do with you
and nothing to do with myself

asking someone to see my worth
will be a request that never
moves past my lips again

did you think i would crumble for the rest of my days ahead
when you exposed your hidden secret to the universe
your lack of concern towards anyone other than yourself
your inability to bring your emotions to the surface
your fear of facing what you ignore day to day
as you watched me succumb towards
your disconnected words
and we both thought that was the end of me
that i saw nothing past the life we created
but you were unaware of the fire that
was spreading inside of me
waiting for this opportunity for explosion

i am trying to remember the day that i
felt nothing for you anymore.
it was a day that was never far behind
when you decided to walk away.
it was early one morning when i laid motionless in bed
piecing through the haziness of my dreams from the
night before. surprised by the emptiness of my thoughts. i
understood what was happening. that was the first morning
i woke up without feeling as though i could not find my
breath. resting my eyes was meant to be my escape from you
yet even in my dreams i found you lurking in every crevice
of my mind. not that morning. i fixed my gaze blankly at a
crack on the ceiling. my chest rising and falling against the
blanket i have now made a home out of. that was the first
morning that i could thank the universe for allowing you to
walk away the way you did. i no longer cursed at the world
for putting me through such an overwhelming heartache.

but here i am this morning. i am lying motionless on my
bed staring at the same crack on the ceiling that i noticed
when i realized you were absent in my dream. how the
forces beyond me knew i needed to take my time to come
to this moment. where this growth could be appreciated. but
here i am wondering how i would react if i spotted you in
a crowd of strangers. would i recognize your face amongst
a sea of the unfamiliar. would the flood of memories from

our past greet me with the urge to speak to you. how one more conversation with you would be enough to ease these lingering thoughts.

for whatever reason the answer to these worries cannot be found. there has to be a reason why after so much time i still hope for you to be okay. moving on does not mean i have forgotten you.

whoever comes next
will have a lot to sort through
but will show me that
love is possible
when times get hard
whoever he is or
whoever she is
will be a breath of fresh air
for the times i searched
for simplicity in all the wrong places

paige cary

you knew that our souls
were not a match together
yet you remained in a place
that did not belong to you

even when you declared
your happiness away from me
you will search for my bravery
in the next person you get a grasp on
just be sure to open yourself up
to avoid days of guilt towards
what you actually want

i have never experienced
such fatigue
all from being alone
without anyone telling me
that i could do more

i assume that they want the same as me
that the warmth of my heart will be all
that it takes for them to want to discover me

i ignore the signs that tell me to protect my spirit
from those that want nothing more than to diminish it

still

i give one piece to him
and i give one piece to her
i give one piece to him
and i give another piece to her
over and over again
hoping someone will hold onto
that part of me that completes me
only instead they drain me from their
reluctancy to get too close to me

i do not think i will ever know what it is like to not wear my heart on my sleeve. my emotions run deep like the ocean and there is so much beauty to revel in when first looked at. the parts that have yet to be discovered are waiting to be seen by eyes that can handle that sort of pressure. perhaps there is nothing wrong with allowing waves of emotion to crash out of me. you see. it is that vulnerability that causes others to drown in front of me. never drifting too far from the surface. and i can no longer fault them for that but rather be patient. as there will be one soul that is willing to lose it all, just to get a glimpse of what others claim as intangible.

how funny is it to have thought
that you would be it for me
that out of all of the creatures
trudging their way through this planet
you would be the one that saw me
to my very last day
to imagine all my years ahead
belonging to your false sense of affection
leaves me frozen in fear
there are too many beating hearts out there
to believe that no one else
would want to love on me
how interesting it is of me
to have given you that much power

paige cary

i am shedding myself
clean from you

i was weak in your eyes
because i hit rock bottom
and decided that the time
had come to face what had
been holding me back
but you were the one
that could not find the strength
to do the same for your own well-being

i go back and forth with my self-destructive habits
one day i desperately need my relationship back
with my one true enemy that knows me too well
i want to feel nothing besides the
razor gliding across my skin
and then the next day a switch goes off inside of me
where my mind is consumed by thoughts of hiding my scars
and instead i bring my fingers to the coils of my curls
and i pull strand after strand off my scalp
flinching each time i rip more of my hair out
this was an easier secret to hide for my sanity
no marks to hide just a flow of curls
to cover this new found desire
i am here and i am aware that it is time to stop
but i need five more minutes with this sudden relief

people come and go
but how they leave
can remain in your heart
longer than anticipated

the night of our last goodbye
left a hole at the bottom of my stomach
drained from my new loss
the only way i could fill the spaces in between
was to fill them with a bit of liquor
i needed to be full of any reminder of you being gone

don't go
please

you gave me one last look
and everything
you were leaving behind
you left a kiss on my cheek
and off you went towards your new life

you told me that
you no longer loved me
that it was too late for us
that in a perfect world
you would be willing
to forget all of this happened
and just go back to how it all started
friends
you did not want to lose me completely
how easy it is for you to pull the rug from right under me
and still expect to have it your way

i can only thank you
for showing me a side
of myself that i pushed away
for so many years
if it was not for this relationship
i would still be silently
fantasizing about a future
with a woman
but now
i am proud of who i like
girls
boys
and anything in between

give yourself room to breathe
it is okay if all you want to do is
cry
or
scream
or
lay in silence with yourself
but at some point
you should know that
you will pick yourself back up
and that will be the start
of your new beginning

i think we forget what we were taught as kids,
treat others the way you want to be treated.
it is a golden rule that seems to slip the minds
of those who are consumed with their own twisted egos.
be cautious towards those people because they are the
type to smile in your face while they
drag your name in the dirt
the minute you are out of their presence.
you show them a glimpse of what it means to be self-aware
and they grab a hold of that sensitivity to take
advantage of what makes you human.
this does not happen immediately though,
you should know that it may be hard to
spot this behavior right away.
they need to breathe all of you in before
they loosen their hold on you,
this is only the beginning of you having
your guard up from person to person.

it is easy for you to reveal the shades that
have been with you through it all.
you are not ashamed nor afraid of the reality
of your story and you should not be,
it is when you give them the chance to see each
part of you that they turn the other way.

they held you close enough to get a taste of what can
be real but their selfishness settles in when they realize
they are unable to give you any love in return.

this is when you reflect
on where you strayed off course
to make them change their mind.
here you are wanting nothing more
than to be seen for the depths of your soul
but instead you tell them to stay and you will change.
you will change for the person who cannot
even be true with themselves.

take a moment to think about this,
you know what love should feel like
even if you have yet to experience it at this point in time.
nothing about that is appeasing or fair to you,
they are not able to find the strength within themselves
to let go of what is not theirs to keep,
all that they saw of you was not enough to
spare you from an unexpected let down.

this is how self-serving individuals
carry themselves in the world,
they push through their days while attaching
themselves to the people who possibly
have what it takes to see all of them at once.
never stopping to take a moment to see if
they are doing themselves a disservice,
they take the pieces of you that satisfy their
needs for that one moment in time
before deciding it is too much to handle on their own
so they bail without giving you a chance
to react to their decision.

when they walk away,
you let them go while holding the door for them.
show them a smile that never breaks away
because you have what it takes to give someone
your whole heart while still making
yourself available to embrace theirs.
you have something many are afraid to express.
you need to protect yourself from people who
do not have your best interest at heart
and believe that there is no such thing as loving too hard.

give yourself room to feel
all the emotions rushing through you
that you so often push to the side
for the sake of another person

you will be okay
you are on the path
towards ultimate happiness
believe that you deserve
all the greatness that the universe
already has in store for you
as it will come before you know it

i never realized how much
i depended on your touch
as the sun peeked through the windows
to quiet our dreams from the night before,
you were close enough to wrap my arms around you
while allowing just a few minutes to go
by before taking on the day.
but now as i turn over from a restless sleep,
it hits me when i look over,
no longer seeing your body sprawled across the sheets.
my days of waking up to you
are now met with finding comfort from
the protection of my own body.

i tell everyone that i am over you
that the idea of you finally being out of my life
is what excites me for my days ahead
but i hang on to any detail that may give away
that you have been thinking of me too
and that there is a piece of you that is missing
now that we no longer call on each other
but instead i inhale the truth of never
crossing paths with you again

paige cary

i listen for the words
that will cling to my skin
to give me the assurance
i need to feel worthy again

i tried many times to get you to see that
i wanted to fix the wall that was building between us.
as soon as i allowed an apology to assure us
it became easier to forget what was happening.
this is how it was supposed to work,
being intertwined with another was work.
you would tell me what i could do better
and you could get lost in your words,
reminding me of what needed attention
an irreversible cycle that never had an end-point
but this was how being in love worked.
seemingly enough you could do no wrong,
perhaps this is why i allowed you to take a walk over me,
somehow you made me blind to all that
was happening in front of me.

somehow
i preferred telling you
i will do better and
i will be better
than have you be a stranger
to my everyday life

but none of this meant anything
i would change if that meant
keeping you around for one more day

being your person was easier
when all we saw in each other
was a friendship that could not be faulted
it was easier to run to you then
without any pressure of
disappointing you for all that i am

i waited to hear from you
days turned into weeks
and that eventually
turned into months
a part of me knew that
i was losing myself
holding onto the past
refusing to let go of the idea
that maybe one day
you might need me again
after all what does that say about me
and does that make me
hopeless to what i once knew
what could be said at this point
if you were to ever reach for me now

i think i always knew that
giving us the space to find ourselves
would eventually be the catalyst
to our predetermined demise

you find the words that pour out of her mind
and you notice how she accepts sadness
the way she protects the madness in her heart
is her way of moving through days that bring chaos
she lures you in with her willingness
to sporadically fall into herself
you may not know what to do with her energy
but you cannot help but gaze in her direction
she will fight many battles before she conforms
to your image of who she should or should not be
somehow she still stands tall when the weight
of the world sits on her sanity
watching her releases something inside of yourself
that you are too afraid to hold onto
when you have survived through trauma
that could have ended you
you figure out how to live for yourself before anyone else
who we are is what our hearts push through our body
when we think we are invisible
after a while
you wake up
you feel her fire because she blatantly
moves herself towards vulnerability

i look for a part of you
in all the new faces
that are now locked in my memory
what is it about them
that can be connected back to you
maybe this is the time to realize
that i am more than
who i was when i was with you

out of all the unexpected goodbye's
that have greeted me
it was the final goodbye
that slipped past your tongue
that shifted something inside of me
the lightness of my heart no longer
served a purpose for me but instead
i found that closing my heart off
will save me for the next visit
cold or not,
no one can hurt you
once you have mastered the art of
self-protection

when it finally comes down to it
the two of us
were never meant to see
each other to the very end

the
recovering...

an open letter to thirteen year old me:

paige...
this is twenty-three year old me acknowledging your thirteen year old self. let me start off by saying that i love you and i wish i could hold your hand every day, just so you know that everything will be okay for you in the end. i want to apologize that i forgot what happened to you that day. it was never my intention to let the situation slip my mind for so many years, but the brain has a way of protecting us even if we do not realize that is what is happening. you were taken advantage of...and i am sorry. years have gone by and the only way i will remember the names of the boys who hurt you is if i open up the yearbook from 2009. i still am not ready to see their faces again. you were at the start of discovering your sexuality with both boys and girls. in high school there is a great amount of pressure when it comes to fitting in with all that you are learning about yourself. i wish more than anything that you were not left behind that day, instead of being left in the presence of the two of them. there is no reason to blame yourself anymore. it was never your fault. they took one look at your innocence and saw the chance to rip it away from you. you took it upon yourself to block out any thought that wanted to remember, but a switch went off within you where you were ready to numb yourself in ways that did more damage than good. i

now know at twenty-three years old that you were searching for protection in all the wrong people. i do not think you understood that you were giving yourself to others to numb the pain you were experiencing from your assault. you were alone in your trauma and i am sorry again. this is the year that self-harming found its way to you which became an on and off battle you had to fight on your own.

if i had the chance to look at you right now, i would tell you that you are enough and you will always be enough… i wish you could see that almost ten years later you can finally look in the mirror without feeling as though you need to hide behind your beautiful chocolate skin. the day does come where you go most days without any makeup because you finally see value within yourself.

thirteen year old paige. you are lost and i love you with every ounce of my being. you are growing into your true self with each day that passes by.

be proud of your efforts.
~ twenty-three year old paige (2018)

to the future paige:

let me start off by saying how proud i am of you. there is not a day that goes by where you should not give yourself a smile for making it as far as you have. i know how easy it is for you to feel lost with your own thoughts. it is scary, especially when you feel as though you are letting others down. i am telling you right now that you are exactly where you need to be. never forget to embrace what you are capable of offering this world. absolutely nobody can take that away from you. you are beautiful, paige. your soul is infectious. you were placed on this earth for a reason. hopefully you are still living by moma's mantra and that is… "don't let anyone steal your joy". moma instilled this into you and chase's mind for a specific reason. i know younger paige tended to dismiss this saying, but i need future paige to listen to those few words. know that people will disappoint you. understand that people may surprise you by their actions, but also accept that the only person you can control is paige michele cary.

be easy on yourself because sometimes life may throw you curveballs that will make you forget all of those things. that is okay. everything that is presented to you in life should be viewed as a blessing in disguise, good or bad. as time pushes forward, i hope you have become at peace with your personal journey and realize that it will never define you. my love for you will continue to grow every single day. if somebody shows you their true colors once, please pay attention, and love yourself first. you know what is acceptable in your life, and you also know all the good that you can offer others. your heart is big, paige. so never apologize for that because there are plenty of people who shut that part of themselves off from the world. that has never been your style, which is an amazing characteristic to have. we all have flaws, i mean we are human so it is a given. embrace your flaws because they make you who you are. if somebody cannot accept your flaws for what they are, then they never deserved to see them in the first place. i just want the best in life for you. your dreams are real. if you stay focused, i believe in my heart that you will see them in front of you sooner than you may have anticipated. believe in your dreams because the only way they will become your reality is if you never let anything or anyone get in the way of them. open your heart out to yourself when you feel alone. use your voice when you feel afraid. most importantly, remember that you will always matter and will forever be enough.

i love you to the moon and back.
~ present paige (2018)

maybe
i have not found what i have been looking for
because i am too open about my truth
maybe
i am paying for what has not come my way
because i put too much on others

let go
of those who
do not see you for all
that you are worth
they never deserved your spirit

you have to love yourself
before anyone can get a glimpse
of all that you have to offer

embrace a new beginning
know that if your world is
changing around you
then you must not question
what has already been set for you

everyday is an opportunity
to grow further into your life purpose

do not allow others
to discourage you from
speaking your truth
your words deserve to be heard
despite the fear others may have
towards their own self

find comfortability with being alone
it does not always have to be scary
you can learn more about yourself
when your mind has a chance to breathe

you feel centered when others are next to you
allow yourself to live freely without the constant
reassurance from those that surround you

do not ask for help
from those who have
made you question their
true intentions
if they have shown you
their true colors
do not be surprised
when you see the same shades
in a new light

sometimes you are your worst critic, but when you are in your most raw state of mind it becomes an indicator that you are exactly where you need to be. it is not easy taking your own advice when you are consumed by your inner turmoils. i not only want to help myself by reading my own words, but you too. it is extremely hard to love yourself every single day. i look into other people's lives and find myself wondering if they really have it all together, or if they are like myself taking all that is thrown my way one day at a time. the moments that pass where we are not tending and loving ourselves turns into a vicious cycle of searching for that feeling of gratification and security in all the wrong places. it is a process that takes an immense amount of patience with yourself. there will be days when all you want to do is succumb to your negative thoughts that are making you question yourself in the first place.

when we find ourselves wallowing in our self-pity, give yourself a moment to...

1. look yourself in the mirror and confront your biggest critic. take the time to sort through your emotions. be sure to ask yourself why you are not giving yourself the love that you know you deserve. remain realistic and know that it may take some time to come to that answer. whatever it is that is

holding you back from doing that should be the reason why you give your undivided attention to those insecurities.

2. understand you are who you are and you only have one life to live. i tend to forget how precious life is at times. it is so easy to get caught up in the drama of our day to day lives. we neglect to take in our surroundings and be appreciative to how far we have truly come. it is exhausting attempting to keep up with other people in hopes of them giving you validation. nobody can tell you about yourself besides you.

3. honestly, be your best friend before anyone else. with that being said, i am not suggesting that another person is incapable of caring for you, but it is close to impossible to have anyone understand you when you are working on that for yourself. it is very easy to give your trust to another person because we all want some kind of reminder that we are doing okay. nothing is wrong with needing to hear that but i urge you to be your own confidant, be your own shoulder to lean on when you feel helpless. by doing that you are actively working on self-love and self-care. you are giving yourself the recognition that you are used to searching for in others.

4. never let go of the people who have your best interest at heart. if you made a mental note as to who those individuals are in your life then they are the people that will be your backbone, your support system, they will continuously be your everything. i understand what my moma means when she says, 'everyone doesn't need to be your friend'. people will disappoint you if you give them the power to do so. if someone shows you who they are once and it hurts, it is a matter of time for when it happens again. do not bring your own spirit down by attempting to mend a friendship or relationship with someone who is okay with letting you down once. it is never worth it.

5. forgive yourself if you have a setback. hannah montana said it best, 'everyone makes mistakes', but it is how we grow from those mistakes that matter. no need to judge yourself if something does not go as planned. as long as you can recognize your mistakes, embrace it for what it is and know that everything else will fall into place when need be.

if you have made it
to see another day
even with the heaviness
around your heart
you were born with
courage

perhaps
we are all in search
for the person who will
entirely shake our world
and make us lose track of time

your pain needs your strength
gravitate towards yourself when
you call upon your own name
whatever you must do
grow into yourself
unapologetically

paige cary

i no longer fear
what the universe
has in store for me
instead
i welcome in the guidance

smile through your toughest days
that sense of pride is contagious

look at all the obstacles
you have managed
to push through
and see that there is
so much life to live

you do not have to be ashamed
of loving someone unconditionally
you have never been afraid of
making others look into themselves
to find their own inner peace

sometimes when you create what you
hope to come into fruition with another person
you end up playing endless mind games
with yourself as to when you will say
what it is that you are feeling

he told me to shave
away the hairs that
bloom delicately
across my body
that no man will
want to be with me
if i am not smooth all over
as if he could have any say
on the way i gracefully
walk in my own skin

to claim your truth
is to gain power
as to what you
will
and
will not
tolerate

for the friends
that decided
i was too much
thank you
for allowing me
to walk alone
your lack of support
forced me to look deeper
and the attention i seeked
was what i desperately
needed for myself
all of your actions
taught me the importance
of enjoying my own company

i know that you are hurting
trust me i do
there are days that never end
and days that leave you spent
i mean it when i say
tomorrow is always around the corner
as always it is a time to start over
if you will give yourself permission
to feel everything you would rather hide behind
you must live in that moment for a while
too often
we are apologetic towards what needs our love
we have to be proud of ourselves for waking up
and taking the first step that leads to becoming a better us

i feel safe with women by my side
as if her very existence is a reminder
that we are a force to come face to face with
the way that we carry the world upon our backs
never once complaining for all that we give
it is the women that stood before me
that made me understand that as long as
air is being pushed into my lungs
there is no comparison to what i am
capable of sharing with this world
all from being a woman

paige cary

your mind has carried many tragedies
all to protect you from the worst
do you realize how fascinating that is

you walking away
is exactly what i needed
to be reintroduced to myself

do not see others
with jealousy
behind your eyes
as their journey
has nothing to do
with your own

you have grown used to
depending on the people
who you think see you
for all that you are
never realizing
you have always had
the strength
to give yourself
that same attention

a life worth living
is full of lessons to be learned
remain willing to embrace
what is meant to come your way
without judgment towards yourself

walking alone
has to be the most rewarding
part of growing up
you think you have all of the answers
and then
something happens to make you question
what you thought to be true
these are the signs that remind you that it is
time to be patient towards what is happening in front of you

paige cary

love what you see
when you lock eyes
with yourself in the mirror

supposedly it is unladylike of me
to walk freely in the skin i am in
because the way my body blooms
is too much for the naked eye

it is better to snip away
the sprouts of life that poke
past the depths of my skin
meaning too much that is seen
can cause controversy on
what it means to be a woman

the development of my body
intimidates those that want
nothing more than to sprawl themselves
across my delicately grown garden

you thought you diminished my spirit
never considering that my spirit was
well and free
way before you caught sight of it

at what age did we stop seeing ourselves as
beautiful
what point in our life made us compare
our every move
to the person that stood next to us

what you accept
is what you will
get in return

i look at you
eager for your acceptance
how is it that you see me
but are not moved to get a hold of me
instead
i get entrapped in my thoughts
on what will never be a reality
for us

i have made it another day without you
but there is still a part of me that wants to see you
to see how far you have come
to see if it is the past that i miss
or just your daily presence
whichever it is
i know deep down that
your distance is for the best

the sweetness
between your thighs
make legs collapse
control that power

share your inner peace
with those who are too
afraid to see their truth
past the outer surface
it is their hearts that
need to be catered to

keep disregarding the power of a woman
it is that sort of attitude that will lead you
down a path of constant disappointment
understand that the women who brought
us into this world have everything that
it takes to tear down mountains from
the power that spills out of them
never allow your mind to think
for one minute that women are weak
we carry the weight of the world on
our shoulders and there is no way
that sort of strength can be
tarnished by a bit of cynicism

you seeing the good in those who have hurt you
does not mean you have suddenly forgotten their actions
it means that you are able to accept
that others have not yet
come face to face with themselves and
that has nothing to do with you
because you have control over nobody but yourself

i want nothing more than to
share my story with someone
and it move something inside of them
all that i have endured
all that i have survived
and all that i have learned
all while wearing my wounds on my sleeve
can push another person to feel validated
within their own tragedies
they can still struggle and be a work in progress
they will look at where i am and know that
you can be handed the worst and still somehow
make it out alive

we have to celebrate
each other without secretly
wanting something in return
be proud when you see someone
thriving in their own world
as they deserve to be proud of their efforts too

paralyzed from ideas that have grown inside of me
never being able to escape the realization that i create the
worries that i allow myself to run wild with
old ways of thinking have led me to a dead end
full of anxieties when i hear words of assurance
that are foreign to my very being
yet these are words that i have longed
to hear from the wrong mouths
that need for validation must be fed
by my own sense of self-love
not knowing that i am deserving
of love will not make love stay
it all comes from within
falling in love with myself
will be my greatest weapon
when dealing with other wandering souls

there is a good chance that she may be the wild one
dancing amidst a sea of quiet souls.
when you first look upon her,
you may feel at a loss of words.
she is unlike anyone you have ever locked eyes on,
you find yourself intrigued by the
beauty that pours out of her.
try not to change the way she navigates
her way through life,
some of the best moments that land in front of us,
are the ones we do not have all the answers to
if we admit it or not.
we all hope to find someone like her once in this lifetime.
someone who is intoxicating by nature,
someone who sparks your curiosity when
unlocking parts of her mind,
conversations that seem to never end because the both of you
are exchanging what it is that excites
and scares you in this life.
at the same time, you are afraid of her seeing all of you.
if you fall trap of that way of thinking,
you will lose her.
you have her already.
you have found someone who will risk it all
to take that leap of faith even when
the unknown is terrifying.
when you see her ready,
be ready with her.

i hope you know how deserving you are of love
love surrounds us every day but when we get caught up
in the flow of life we tend to become blind to this
sometimes our past makes us afraid to accept love
when it looks us directly in the eye
open your heart up towards what scares you

i hope you know that there is someone who is drifting
through their own days in search for
a love that belongs to you
the part of yourself that you claim as unlovable will be
the part of you that ignites something within someone else
where you have been is not where you are going

i hope you know that there is no
reason for you to hold onto
the fear of expressing your deepest emotions
the right person will watch you do so in awe
i hope you meet yourself halfway
believe that all that is meant for you
is coming your way

sometimes you will find yourself gravitating
towards the wrong people
it is frustrating to you because you have
worn yourself down to the bone
in attempt to please a person who cannot
comprehend your intensity
a lot of people do not have the drive
to dig deep when it comes to
exploring the mind of another
despite the voice in your head
that is telling you to be proud of your truth
you still end up being the one that
knocks down your own worth
the person looking back at you urges
you to reveal parts of yourself
that requires the unveiling of the ugly truth
on why you operate the way that you do
somehow once your truth is heard
you are now categorized as being too much
there is confusion that consumes your insides
when it comes to the next person
do you speak from the heart
do you show that emotions is what drives you forward
do you be your authentic self

yes
yes
and yes
if somebody cannot handle who you are as a person
know that there is nothing wrong with that
you should not have to teach someone how to love you
it is rare to find someone who loves as effortlessly as you do
do not diminish that part of you in hopes of being seen
completely

paige cary

show up for yourself
and watch how the rest follows

you spend too much time contemplating
all of the what if's that will greet you in this life
some of those worries may never make it to your reality
live in the moment for once with a sense of curiosity
laugh when you cannot seem to bring a smile to your face
and remember to be patient
you will not have the answers to
everything that comes your way
but when you give yourself room to remain open
you will realize that you can handle more
than you give yourself credit for

paige cary

allow me to get lost in you

your body responds
before your mind understands
what is happening to you
honor your intuition
when it calls for your
attention

if you want to help someone
do so from the bottom of your heart
without any sort of expectation back
as there will be a time when you will
not have all of the answers and will
need all the guidance to discover
what you do not know on your own

sometimes i sit in silence for hours
without finding any urge to move
this is how i deal with my depression and anxiety
i become stagnant by the power of my own mind
and the thing is
i know i am able to fight the negativity off
but sometimes my voice is not as
confident as its combative peers
i am able to convince myself that i am
not worthy enough all while
the tears that paint a masterpiece along my
skin is the confirmation to just that
i must agree with what my mind is trying to
get me to see if this is what happens
but maybe me picking up this pen and
spreading it across these pages is me
fighting back

i am holding back my tears right now
why must i do that to myself
why must i ignore my emotions
this has become the pattern of my life
i am desperate
i am desperate for answers
desperate for a clear understanding
of my chemically imbalanced mind
there is no way to explain this feeling
my heart rapidly beating
against the walls of my chest
is it really my heart though
or is it just me
a version of myself doing anything and everything
for me to see what i am worth
the innocence of this girl is apparent

this girl is brave
this girl is care-free
this girl is a survivor
this girl will do whatever it takes
for the woman on the outside
to be reminded of who she is

together these two girls can be free
free of the trauma
free of the anxiety
and free of the constant depression
these two girls will only survive for each other
and just be

i will be free

the moment you sit back
to take in all that you have
you will no longer feel
unsatisfied towards what
is not yours just yet

some days are easier than others

paige cary

i do not cry
for the attention
these tears fall because
i no longer want to
fault myself for
having emotions
that i am still
trying to get a grasp on

wish happiness on the individuals
that crossed your path and
made you second guess your
purpose on this earth and
forgive their wrongdoing
to release you from their
hold on your chance
to move forward in life

but we all want to be happy
at the very end of time
however the idea of happiness
has been formulated to look
a certain way in our eyes
when happiness is what
we believe it to be and
my sense of happiness
will not be identical to your own

i am so much more than a woman
who managed to make it out alive
i am a warrior who is unafraid
to scream at the top of her lungs
a body that is filled with rage
from the destruction that was placed upon it
there is so much of me that needs to be seen
so pay attention to the story that unfolds in front of me

whatever comes next for me
i want to remain present with myself
as there is nothing that can hold me down
because this life of mine
is mine to keep

quit blaming yourself for feeling hopeless at times
every emotion that comes from within you is valid
too often do we look down on ourselves for feeling

but we need to know that
the only person that can
bring pure satisfaction
into our lives is ourselves
there is no way we can be lost
when we create what brings us joy

what is that makes paige happy?
i was asked this every single day while hospitalized
and each time i mumbled without an ounce of confidence
that i did not know how to answer such a question.
just because it was a new day did not mean
i would suddenly know what to say.
but i never felt judged for not knowing how to
answer that simple question on
what is it that makes paige happy?

but it was when i was left alone,
laying in the darkness of my room,
staring at the empty walls surrounding me,
that something clicked inside of me.
this happiness that they asked me about
said goodbye to me when ripped away at thirteen.
that girl who still played board games occasionally
and that girl who still found herself playing
with dolls from time to time,
or wanting to spend hours playing video
games with her older brother.
i realized that i have always longed to have
the simplicity of those days back.

my days in the hospital are now coming to an end
and again i am asked the same question as before
what is it that makes paige happy?
before i gave the same answer as previous times
i looked my therapists in the eyes and told her
i am searching for that now,
and although i may not know what that looks like
i am positive that i will find it sooner than later.

for so long i placed my perception of
happiness onto the life of another
and never realized i was just giving
my worth away to people,
who only wanted to embrace certain parts of me.
and i lost myself by doing that
and i always found myself disappointed
in another person's actions.
i believed that someone could make me love me
the way i thought i deserved to be loved.

i exhausted my energy trying to get anybody
to show unconditional love towards me
this is what i thought happiness was
supposed to look like for paige.

to be honest i think we are all searching
for something bigger than ourselves.
whatever is happening to us today,
right now in this moment,
is never enough.
and i am left wondering when that all changed
not just for myself but for us all.
how is it that being alive is not enough
to keep us happy for a lifetime?

so now it is time to ask myself the same question that
has been mentioned countless times
before without an answer
what is it that makes paige happy?
and i think i know what that looks like for me now.

the day i was able to look in the mirror
and hold eye contact with myself,
appreciating all the beauty that i for so
long wanted to be stripped clean of.
that is what happiness looks like to me.
the day i was able to say what i will and
will not tolerate from a person,
that is what happiness looks like to me.

we have control on what it is that makes us happy
and the second you have to ask yourself
if the feelings that are swarming inside of you are real,
stop yourself and ask why they would not be.
ask yourself what it is that makes you happy
and go from there.

accepting change can be a difficult task to overcome
even when you try to have control over what is happening
around you or within you
change can be the piece that has been missing all along
and that alone takes time to understand

believe me when i say
i know i am not the easiest to love
i am a woman who has a lot to say
and sometimes what needs to be said
is also hard to hear but above it all
i am a woman who strives to be different
i do not want to be like anybody else
something inside of me ignites
when i open up my heart to another
whoever it is that comes my way
will feel this energy right away
and either you become one with my being
and survive through the strength
that flows out of me
or you crumble at my knees knowing that you
do not have what it takes to walk next to me
until then i will walk alone as i am the only one
who can handle every part of me

we see no issue in judging the faults of others
but rarely find the time to reflect
on how we could be better
for whatever reason it is so easy
to lose ourselves in someone
as if living for us it too much to ask for
i find myself running in circles over and over again
trying to become this image that i
believe is necessary to be seen

there are plenty of eyes that are eager to
examine what is sacred to you
but very few have the capacity to hold
onto all that you can give at once
so of those that are lucky enough to see that part of you
keep them close as they are hard to find

love me when i cannot find the strength to
give myself the love you know i deserve.
love me when i have turned my back
on you to sob silently to myself,
terrified that if you see me like that,
the real me,
you would turn the other way without looking back.
when the tears have stained themselves dry across my face,
an image i would not want others to see,
be patient and love me then.

love me when my anxiety and
depression gain a hold of me.
love me when i would rather sit in
silence than hold a conversation.
love me when i ramble on about the
same topic for the tenth time
but you cannot find it within yourself to tell me so.
love me when i tell you there is not a set date for
when i will feel better about my trauma.
love me when i find more comfort in opening
up to my therapist than with you.
love me when i find the courage to share my past with you
but struggle to do so because my past can
make the present me want to hide.
love me when racing thoughts fill my mind and
leave me on the brink of letting it all out,
be patient and love me then.

love me when i tell you i want to be a better person,
a better daughter, a better sister, a better
friend, a better human being.
none of that will happen overnight,
i cannot be my best self at all times.
all i can say is that i will always try my best.
love me when you see the effort i am putting
into growing into a better woman.
love me in my darkest moments because i
promise that love will be reciprocated .
love me when i am using every part
of me to keep it together.
love me when nobody else has the energy
to deal with my mixed emotions.
please show up for me and love me then.
love me when i least expect it.
believe me when i say i will not always be beautiful.
i will not be picture perfect at all times.
the girl you first fell in love with
will not always be around,
but if you promise to love me then,
and all the days ahead
and if you give me that chance
i swear i will love you then too.

if you are hurting to the point of seeking validation
from any person who will listen to you
do yourself a favor and take the advice
from someone who spent too much time
hoping to hear all the things
i wish i could say to myself
you may have to learn the hard way
but it is nobody's responsibility
to patch up your hidden wounds
your pain needs to be tended to
by the person who has walked through
the journey of life with you every step of the way
that person is you
you are the only one who can save yourself
and it is not an easy task to accomplish
but anything is possible
so do yourself the favor
and look in the mirror
and tell yourself that you are here to stay

i see hope behind your eyes
that somewhere way past
what others see on the surface
is a place that is blocked off
for only a select few
if you had the patience
to allow me to work through those barriers
maybe we would surprise ourselves
as to what reveals itself

how do you expect to experience
all that life has to offer
if you refuse to put yourself out there
allow something to switch inside of you
by taking an unforeseen risk
if that leads to failure
then so be it
lessons are meant to push us forward
but what if you do the unordinary for yourself
and discover the missing piece to your story
embrace the unknown

some people walk in your life
for a reason
a season
or a lifetime
all serve a purpose for your growth
and you should know that it is not
the end of the world if the time has come
to shut the door on a situation that once
gave you an immense amount of happiness
when you pick yourself back up
you will see that there is
another story for you to understand
that right through that door
something greater is awaiting your arrival

small accomplishments
deserve the same amount
of praise as the bigger strides
each one happens to be the
reason that your story continues

remind yourself everyday
that you have a purpose here
if there is a moment of self-doubt
do not hold judgment in your heart
rather tell yourself that every negative feeling
that you may have towards yourself is only temporary
and above all this too shall pass
there is something captivating about
strengthening your mind with positivity
allow that to wash over you and
pay attention to the growth that follows

to the young girls that look at their
reflection without appreciation,
you deserve to know a million times and
more that your beauty is one of a kind.
when you came into this world you knew nothing
of the damaging standards of beauty
that you will soon be introduced to but you
must be your biggest supporter when you
begin to compare yourself to others.
you have to look at the skin you
live in and show unconditional love to the
parts of you that make you want to hide.
every inch of you deserves love and
dedication. it is then that you will see
you are who you are and spending your
energy on how to be different will only
lead you down a path of constant disappointment.

tell me something
have you ever seen someone
as twisted as me
there are times that my chaos
takes over you with no warning
but despite the truth in that
you still find yourself
wrapped away in the fury of my wrath
i have made it impossible to see what
has always been in front of you
so again tell me something
what will it take for you to admit that
you too dance in this same chaotic mess

you are making me think differently
not just about myself but i have noticed
my thoughts shifting towards how i look
at the situations that now land in my lap
you are making me feel like a girl
that just discovered what it means to
have a rush of emotions take over me
the butterflies that scatter themselves
along the walls of my stomach
yet there is nowhere for them to escape to
the moment those creatures catch a glimpse
of anything else past their current barriers
their wings will spread and there will be no walls
to stop them from flying away
i am not afraid of vulnerability when there is
so much of your mind to explore in depth
it is as if we got a glimpse of one another's eyes
and something inside me stopped for a moment
could this be why there is hesitancy floating between us
is the reason i am already feeling something because
all i have ever wanted was to feel alive with another soul

i am not a lab rat for experiments
these pills that are meant to fix me
only leave me feeling like a version
of myself that does not exist
but here i am staring at this bottle that is supposed
to have all the answers for my depressive episodes
or the ability to quiet my rambunctious mind
one tiny pill will solidify it all for me
instead i look at all the pills that have been
placed in me and more than anything
i feel ready to cut the ties
my happiness is what i make of it
i do not want my happiness to rely on a medication
that must be taken each time i open my eyes for a new day
the happiness that i crave comes from looking at myself
and reminding myself that i can do
whatever i put my heart to
the love that i am learning to accept for myself
now pours out of me the moment that i
battle these self-loathing thoughts
these good moments will not be every day
but my resilience will be forever

you give yourself zero room
to heal
to grow
to learn
from past mistakes
to become a version of yourself
that is unstoppable
if you seek to hurt others

you have grown used to plastering a smile on your face
reminding everyone that you are doing just okay
but the minute that they let go of your gaze is
when you struggle to bring that same joy to yourself.
perhaps you feel as though your inner thoughts
have cut off all of your circulation and your ability
to vocalize what is scattered along
the corners of your mind.
so you eventually find yourself in this
cycle that gets no recognition
but you cannot reach your full potential
being afraid of vulnerability.
there will be times when you feel
compelled to express yourself
because somewhere within you there
was a door that creeped open
that held your self-confidence but for
whatever reason you could not see it.
you see, there will be moments that the
door to confidence is anything
but possible to open and you will feel
exhausted from the amount

of times that you tried to see the possibility of it all again.
i am telling you now that you are
stronger than you may think
and your persistency to find confidence
is not to be ignored.
think about it.
the times that you have felt discouraged
towards moving forward
but something happens that stops you in your tracks
big or small,
whatever it was somehow brought
that smile back to your face.
you did not expect it to be that simple but it is,
allow that to be the reminder that
centers your intrusive thoughts.
every emotion that washes over us is temporary.
the lessons that we learn throughout the journey of life,
will stay with us much longer.
you deserve to smile.

i do not want to wake up one day
still fantasizing about what could have been
i do not want to look back one day
wishing i found the courage to say how i feel
the thought of you is what puts me at ease
but what if i speak up
and the words that escape from inside me
burn a hole into your mind
leaving you numb on how to act with me
maybe i should just ask
ask you if you too
have felt something move in you

it is close to impossible
to be near you and suddenly
stop myself from wanting you

say you were told that tomorrow
would be your last day,
would you finally allow the walls
that you have built up to collapse
all at once at your feet
and you just live
live without thinking of what comes next
or would you still convince yourself
that there is too much risk in doing that
ask yourself
what can make today be the day
that slows down your thinking
and you just go
you go for what you want
you go for who you love
you go as if nothing in this world
can convince you to stop
why can that day not be today

my chaotic story has navigated me
to the only voice that matters here
and that is my own
there is no space inside of me
that can be filled with harmful thinking
not towards myself that is
i am who i am
and i no longer apologize for that
take me or leave me
but i will remain standing

paige cary

i whispered to the moon
what it is that i see
when i look at you
but i told her to protect
those nightly confessions
as anything that makes it to light
can be misconstrued to nothing
if those words are not shared just right
so i will keep you as my secret
until i have seen you through the night

i think it is you that makes the most sense
because all the others force me to be
a version of myself that i do not recognize

do not be afraid at all that you can be
the flaws that you deem as unlovable can be
the reasons another soul is in awe of you
what is yours is yours to keep
so wear it as your truth because everything
that is meant for you is up to you
remind yourself that you can still grow
with a fire burning in your belly because
you are the warrior of your own story
while still remaining as the fairest of them all
it is the warmth of your soul that helps
the world around you see what strength looks like
set yourself free from any burden that you may carry
and become everything you never imagined yourself to be

to the boys who assaulted me at thirteen and nineteen years old:

it is taking everything in me to write out these words. i have wondered countless times if it is worth saying anything at all. this will never get to you, but i have come to the realization that this is my way of 'letting go.' even when i say that, i begin to shake my head at myself. how am i supposed to let go of what the two of you did to me at thirteen and what you did to me at nineteen? i am a statistic at the end of the day. i mean, we all fall under some sort of statistic, but i want you to see some that pertain to me specifically.

1. every 98 seconds, an american is sexually assaulted
2. a majority of child victims are between the ages of 12-17 years old
3. 48% of sexual assault victims were sleeping, or performing another activity at home
4. ages 12-34 are the highest risk years for rape and sexual assault
5. women 18-24 who are college students are three times more likely than women in general to experience sexual violence
6. 94% of women who are raped experience ptsd
7. 33% of women who are raped contemplate suicide
8. 73% of women who are raped attempt suicide

i was raped at thirteen years old by the both of you who at the time were eighteen. it has been about ten years and i have pushed the images of your faces so far behind the darkest corners of my mind that the only way i would remember is if i pull out my yearbook. i was raped again at nineteen by you, the person i was dating for a short three months. something detached itself from me when you violated me while asleep. i am turning twenty-four in just two weeks and i am reaching the point where i can say out loud that i was indeed raped, but more importantly i have made it another year alive. my teenage years were spent doing anything in my power to be out of the skin i was in. i never understood why i could never look at myself in the mirror without cringing, or say anything positive about myself. in my heart i knew where it stemmed from, but i was too embarrassed to admit the pain that i carried around with me. my introduction with intimacy was violent, and let me keep reminding you that this was at thirteen years old. the start of my teenage years began with a rape and the ending of my teenage years closed with a rape. ironic. i have spent the past decade searching for love and affection in all the wrong places. i had this idea that in order for me to be 'okay' with my assaults i could just become more sexual. numb up my emotions and give what was taken from me to anyone that gave me the right amount of attention to avoid my reality as much as possible. just like most things that tend to get bottled up, that method for coping only works temporarily. there will be a time where it all lands right back onto your lap waiting for your acceptance.

i dealt with the trauma when rock bottom welcomed me with open arms. my mental illnesses had gotten so out of control that i thought the only way out of the chaos, that was my mind, would be to end it. i am saying this not only to let go of any uneasy feelings towards the three of you, but allowing myself to forgive as well. i never wanted to believe in the saying, 'you can forgive but never forget.' individually the three of you took away my innocence, my self-confidence, and my trust in men. you were not able to steal away my inner strength. you all took a piece of me away with you, but you also gave me the chance to discover how to pull myself out of despair. none of this happened over night as you know. ten years of running away from my truth. i am here to tell you the future is waiting for me with open arms.

i no longer give you guys the power to steal my joy. you never deserved it. i give myself full freedom to acknowledge the past as the past. i just hope that there is not another me in your life. i would never wish my experiences on my worst enemy.

i wish you the best.
paige

to my brother:

you are my best friend and better half all in one. there is never a day that goes by where i do not think about how lucky i am to be your baby sister. the both of us together is a lot to take in. i mean that in the best way possible. the way that we see the world has not always been the same. as time pushes forward i recognize how the way we think individually is indescribable. we lean on each other for guidance. you continuously show me the importance of believing in myself. the years of me feeling ashamed of my dark skin was mentally exhausting. all of our conversations that revolved around me building up my confidence has given me the strength to finally look at myself in the mirror with a genuine smile. i now can appreciate my beauty due to your encouragement. sometimes i do not think you realize how thankful i am for you for pushing me towards happiness for all these years. it was you who heard the pain in my voice when i was at my rock bottom. you listened to me when i said i was lost. it was you who told moma and daddy that i needed to come home to be put into a rehab program for my mental health. it was you who was living in another state and called the police when i attempted to take my own life.

it is you who repeatedly saves me and fights for me to see my worth when i cannot seem to find it myself. i am thankful to be alive because of you my chasey bear. i believe in your dreams. your mind will shape the mind of others in this world. i want to give you the same support that was given to me for so many years.

thank you from the bottom of my heart.

pp

to my moma:

where do i even begin? how am i supposed to find the words to describe how much you mean to me? i feel as though there are no words that can capture the amount of love i have for you. to be honest, sometimes i forget how blessed i am to have a relationship with my mother, especially the one that we share. the thought of not having you in my life scares me down to my core because over the years you have grown to be my number one confidant. i think it was difficult for my younger self to recognize how much you always had my back. all of my teenage years were spent doing anything in my power to be a disobedient daughter. for whatever reason i thought that all of the answers to the world had already been given to me, and i could never be wrong. you wanted nothing more for me to see all that i am worth and to stop with my self-destructive behavior before it got the best of me. more than anything i wanted to share my innermost turmoils that i carried with me. i refused to allow you, daddy, or chase to understand how badly i was hurting. i apologize over and over again at the times i have left you concerned for my well-being and future. now that i have made it into my 24th year of living, i cannot help but thank you for your guidance and wisdom. moma, we are more alike than we ever admit, but it is the truth. there is nothing that i cannot share with you at this point in my life.

i will always need you, and you need to know that you have changed chase and i's lives by being our mother. your good spirit is contagious to all that gets a glimpse at you. some may be envious of your personality because you know how to bring a smile to anybody's face that you lock eyes with. i feel like i am winning every single day for getting to have you as my moma. please remember to tell yourself that you are deserving of love and admiration to yourself. you never think twice about being there for the ones you love, and it is time that you give that same dedication to yourself. you have earned it. tell yourself that all throughout the day, so you can never forget it.

thank you for everything.
and thank you for being you.

i love you more.

paigey-paige

to my daddy:

you are the best human being that i have the privilege of knowing. my introduction to what unconditional love from a man should look like came from you. there is not a day that goes by where i do not feel lucky for all that you have given me and our family over the years. there are times that i feel guilty for not being in the position in life to give you all that you have given me. it would never come out of your mouth that you would expect such a gesture, but i never expected to be given the life that you have provided for me. there will be a day that i will repay you for everything. it took me a long time to get an understanding of the way your mind works. you are a man of few words. this is the complete opposite of me, which you have seen the more that i grow into myself. when you do reveal the truth, it is direct and at times intimidating. you know that i have always had a hard time hearing the ugly truth when it is needed, but you have never been afraid to lay it on me because you have always known that i have it in me to pull myself out of anything. i said the same to moma, but i wish i shared my trauma with you sooner than i did. i was embarrassed for years, and i was finally met face to face with hitting rock bottom. never in my life could i have ever imagined wanting to leave this world behind. you saw me reach that point to which you took on the role as my father and protected me.

i was silently suffering for ten years. i broke that silence by attempting to leave all that i have ever known. that was not an option, so you put me in rehab. i am blessed. i am grateful beyond measure for you showing me the beauty of life and allowing me to get the help that i desperately needed. i love you for giving me the strength to pick myself up and encouraging me to move forward. there are people that have never known the feeling of having support from a father. i cannot imagine a life with that as my reality. you have shown me the importance of never allowing an obstacle to hinder me from getting to where i am meant to be. i will take that with me for the rest of my life. i believe in myself because you have never given up on me.

thank you for being the best man that i have ever known.

paigey-paige

FIND HELP

If you or someone you know self-harms, please get help right now!

Crisis Text Line: crisistextline.org; Text 741-741

S.A.F.E. Alternatives: selfinjury.com; 1-800-DONTCUT

To Write Love On Her Arms: twloha.com

Mental Health America (MHA):
mentalhealthamerica.net/self-injury

If you or someone you know suffers from depression or anxiety, please get help right now!

Teen Lifeline: teenlifeline.org; 1-800-248-8336 (TEEN)

National Alliance On Mental Illness (NAMI): nami.org

Teen Mental Health: teenmentalhealth.org

If you or someone you know is suicidal, please get help right now!

National Suicide Prevention Lifeline: suicidepreventionlifeline.org; 1-800-273-8255

If you or someone you know has been raped or sexually abused, please get help right now!

Rape, Abuse, Incest National Network (RAINN): 1-800-656-HOPE (4673)

If you or someone you know has been domestically abused, please get help right now!

National Domestic Violence Hotline: 1-800-799-SAFE (7233)

appreciation

you have seen the pages of my diary. you have seen my heart. and for that i am grateful. thank you for tuning into my journey. thank you for allowing my words to become a part of your world. it never occurred to me that i would find so much comfort getting lost with only a pen and page to hold me steady. at a very young age i became the master of silence. how could my own tragedies be worth expressing to anyone other than myself. i was compelled to speak up when i finally took the time to open my eyes to the love and support i had beside me all along. something clicked inside when the realization that my voice mattered hit me. the story that is rooted in me can unlock a place in your own heart that is in desperate need of light. i am asking you to trust in yourself now as i give myself to you. you may be tired. you may feel alone. but i am here to tell you that i am with you. there is a peaceful new beginning waiting to meet you eye to eye if you decide to push love into your own heart. i promise you that nothing can stand in our way if we remain one with ourselves.

about the book

a paige in my diary is a collection of poetry.
broken into four segments.
the suffering.
the colliding.
the wandering.
and the recovering.
step inside the walls that protect the entireity of my soul.
you will find the discovery of my sexuality.
you will find my secrets that are surrounded by sexual abuse.
you will find my will to be loved back.
but most importantly.
you will find the drive i have to survive.

about the author

paige cary is a los angeles based artist. *a paige in my diary* is paige's debut poetry book. she was introduced to the world of art at the age of ten when her parents put her in her first acting class. moving into her teenage years is when paige started carrying a journal wherever she went. shortly after receiving her bachelors degree in acting, she had no other choice but to deal with her mental health. after spending time in rehab, paige spent 2017 and 2018 falling deep into her writing to bring this poetry book to life. the collection of writing you will read in *a paige in my diary* will hopefully start a conversation on topics that many feel ashamed to bring up themselves. paige is currently working on her second collection of poetry to publish in the near future. she looks forward to growing into her art further over the years.

follow paige on instagram at paigemichelex

follow paige on twitter at paige_n_my_diary

follow paige at paigecary.com

CPSIA information can be obtained
at www.ICGtesting.com
Printed in the USA
FSHW020707090220
66967FS